AI-Driven Gaming

How Artificial Intelligence is Shaping Video Games

Table of Contents

Chapter 1. Introduction

Welcome to a fascinating odyssey into the world of artificial intelligence (AI) and gaming! In this special report, "AI-Driven Gaming: How Artificial Intelligence is Shaping Video Games," we delve into the extraordinary revolution AI has ignited in the gaming industry. We've distilled complex technologies into a lucid and engaging narrative, breaking down the subject matter into digestible insights. From shaping more lifelike Non-Player Characters (NPCs) to revolutionizing game design and improving player experience, we explore how AI is fundamentally changing the way we play and perceive video games, and why it matters. This journey transcends the realm of gaming and provides a glimpse into the future of interactive entertainment and beyond. Whether you're a gaming enthusiast, a tech-savvy individual, or simply curious about the future of technology, this report is an essential compass guiding you through the complex yet thrilling landscape of AI-driven gaming. It's more than just a report—it's an investment in understanding the future of one of the fastest-growing industries on the planet!

Chapter 2. Unveiling the Game: An Introduction to AI in Gaming

A new era is unfolding in the world of video games, with artificial intelligence (AI) taking the helm. To truly grasp the incredible revolution that AI has sparked, it's crucial first to understand what this technology is and how it functions within the context of gaming.

AI, at its core, is computer systems or software designed to emulate human intelligence. This includes learning (the accumulation of information and rules for using it), reasoning (using rules to reach conclusions), perception (interpreting the sensory inputs), and language understanding (comprehending spoken and written language).

2.1. The Advent of AI in Video Games

With the first video game, 'Spacewar!', being developed in 1962, video games have drastically evolved over the years. The first use of AI in gaming surfaced in the 1970s with arcade classics like 'Pong'.

Over the years, artificial intelligence has been used to boost the complexity of video games, emulating human-like behaviour and creating a more interactive environment. Initially, the AI in games was rudimentary, mainly used in limiting computer-controlled characters. These characters operated within the bounds of pre-set complete behavioural patterns which were quite easy to foresee after several game rounds.

The true turning point emerged in the late 90s, with real-time strategy game—'StarCraft', which introduced a more sophisticated approach to AI. Now, AI could analyze, plan, and even react to human player actions, marking the birth of a more dynamic and interactive era in gaming.

2.2. AI Technologies in Gaming

In the domain of video gaming, two significant types of artificial intelligence are utilized: general AI and narrow AI. General AI is the comprehensive intelligence found in humans that exhibits versatility and adaptability, while narrow AI displays proficiency at performing a specific task where it's programmed.

In video games, narrow AI is predominant. This type of AI is task-specific, for instance, controlling non-player characters (NPCs), pathfinding for characters to evade obstacles, or generating new levels in games for accentuating replay value.

Some widespread AI techniques used in gaming include:

- Finite State Machines (FSM): The earliest AI component in games, FSM represents AI behaviour as states. Each state has defined actions, and changes from one state to another are triggered by conditions.

- Utility-based systems: These AIs allow characters to make decisions based on the action's utility. They rank all possible actions and select the one with the highest value.

- Machine Learning (ML): An application of AI, ML allows game characters to learn from data input without being explicitly programmed. It's utilized optimally for training NPCs and evolving them based on player interaction patterns.

2.3. The Impact of AI on Players and NPCs

AI functions not only in the creation of lifelike environments or impressive graphic renderings, but it is now pushing the envelope further by making NPCs who can react intelligently to human players, learn from them and even communicate sensitively in human-like language. This transformation brings a whole new level to the gaming experience.

The use of AI in crafting NPCs has added complexity to games and made them far more engaging. AI-led dialogues simulate near-human responses, characters with learning abilities adapt over time and gameplay, AI-driven NPCs making their unique decisions, all contribute to imitating real-world scenarios and enhance the overall user experience.

Some games even leverage AI to customize difficulty level as per individual player behaviour, slotting them into 'buckets' based on skill levels, thus assuring every player an optimised gaming experience.

Simultaneously, on the multiplayer game platforms, AI bots imitate human players, competing against themselves when human players are unavailable, testing the game and providing game designers with invaluable insights.

2.4. AI in Game Design and Development

AI has steadily taken up essential roles not only in gaming but also in the process of game design and development. Procedural Content Generation (PCG) is an AI-based technique where game content like levels, maps, items, quests, or even entire game rules are generated programmatically.

PCG has many benefits. It helps cut down on manual labour and production costs, increase replay value by generating new content each time, offer infinite variants and keep the game environment dynamic. Popular games like 'No Man's Sky' generate entire universes using PCG.

AI, particularly machine learning, is emerging as a handy tool in playtesting. With AI-led automation, it is possible to simulate thousands of playthroughs in a fraction of the time it would take human testers, identifying bugs and balance issues rapidly.

2.5. AI and the Future of Gaming

Artificial Intelligence has revolutionized the gaming space, but this is just the beginning. As technology advances, games will become more immersive, intuitive, and personalized. With the advent of technologies like augmented reality, virtual reality, and developments in AI, the gaming industry is poised to transcend into an era of unprecedented sophistication and engagement.

In summary, the integration of AI in gaming has rendered games more complex, engaging, and closer to reality, with massive improvements in NPC behaviour, game design, player customization, as well as aiding game development. AI's impact is not limited to the player's experience but extends to developers and how games are shaped. The complex and thrilling landscape of AI-driven gaming promises an exciting future, not only in terms of entertainment but also its implications for human-computer interaction and artificial intelligence at large.

Chapter 3. The AI Evolution: A Historical Overview in Gaming

To appreciate the current state of AI in gaming, we need to trace back its roots to the dawn of video games. AI in video games emerged as early as the 1950s, albeit in a much more rudimentary form than what we are accustomed to today.

3.1. The Infancy: 1950s - 1970s

The genesis of integrating AI into gaming can be attributed to the 1951 game of 'Nim', designed by Ferranti. It's a simple strategy game wherein the goal was to prevent being the player to pick up the last object. In a sense, this AI mimicked strategy playing. The next significant breakthrough came in the form of 'Spacewar!', created in 1962, where the players controlled spaceships and attempted to destroy each other. Although these examples might seem rudimentary by today's standards, they laid the groundwork for the role of AI in gaming.

In the 1970s, games like 'Pong' and 'Space Invaders' took advantage of improved technology to create a more interactive and engaging AI environment. Though the AI was algorithmic, it gave players the illusion of playing against an intelligent opponent. Simultaneously, text-based games like 'Adventure' and later 'Zork' presented players with AI entities that were capable of interpreting player inputs and responding in a way that created a semblance of intelligence.

3.2. A Step-Up: 1980s - 1990s

Entering the 1980s, the incorporation of AI in gaming started to become more prevalent. Developers aimed at using AI to create richer, more immersive worlds that would challenge and engage the player on a whole new level. Games of this era introduced rudimentary pathfinding algorithms, decision trees, and more complex rules for NPCs, enhancing in-game interactions. One notable example is 'Pac-Man', where each ghost had its own set of behaviors, which created varied and unpredictable gameplay.

The 1990s heralded an era of experimentation with more complex AI routines in gaming. Games like 'Civilization', 'Black & White', and 'The Elder Scrolls' series brought NPCs who could make complex decisions and had rudimentary personalities. This period laid the foundation for the AI we see in contemporary video games.

3.3. The Boom: 2000s - Present

With technological advancements, the evolution of AI in the 2000s transformed the gaming experience dramatically. Games became more sophisticated, requiring AI not only to simulate human-like opponent behavior but also to create rich and immersive in-game worlds. 'Half-Life' revolutionized gaming AI with NPCs having the ability to analyze the environment, communicate with each other and coordinate attacks. 'F.E.A.R' set a new benchmark for AI with sophisticated enemy tactics based on the player's actions. Simulations became increasingly complex, with 'The Sims' revolutionizing the concept of creating and controlling life.

The rising popularity of MMORPGs like 'World of Warcraft' required AI to manage a multitude of tasks like interactive environments, responsive NPCs with distinct behaviors, and handling an enormous quantity of player data.

The 2000s also saw the growth of neural networks and machine learning, significantly influencing the role of AI in video games. Techniques like reinforcement learning allowed AI to learn optimal strategies through gameplay. 'AlphaGo' from Google's DeepMind demonstrated these technologies' exciting potential when it defeated the world champion Go player in 2016.

3.4. The Future: AI and Gaming Beyond

Looking ahead, AI is expected to play an even more substantial role in video games, creating adaptive gameplay that reacts and evolves based on player actions. Games like 'Hello Neighbor' are showcasing these capabilities, with an AI opponent that learns from the player's tactics and adjusts its strategies in response.

Technologies such as procedural content generation (PCG), which uses algorithms to produce game content like terrain, levels, and items dynamically, are expected to become more prevalent, fundamentally altering how games are designed and played. Machine learning will further enhance NPC behavior, making virtual characters even more lifelike.

Through advancements in AI, video games are destined to be more immersive, challenging, and adaptive than ever before, providing experiences that can truly react and evolve based on how we play.

In conclusion, the journey of AI in gaming has been nothing short of exciting. From its humble beginnings in the 1950s to the ground-breaking innovations of today, AI has steadily transformed the gaming landscape into what we see today. As we continue to push the boundaries of technology and machine learning, there's no limit to what the future holds for AI in gaming.

Chapter 4. Inside AI Characters: The Creation of Non-player Characters

The creation of non-player characters (NPCs) is a pivotal aspect of gaming, demanding intricate design and development. Coupled with artificial intelligence, NPCs are demonstrating a newfound depth, presenting as lifelike characters with distinct identities and adaptable interactions.

4.1. The Evolution of Non-Player Characters

Tracing the history of NPCs, we note their function was initially quite basic—primarily as plot pushers and game enhancers. An early example includes the ghosts in Pac-Man or the guards in Metal Gear. They had limited interactions and predictable patterns. Over years, NPCs have evolved significantly, exhibiting greater complexity and autonomy, thanks to advancements in AI.

AI infuses life into NPCs, enabling them to interact meaningfully with the gaming environment and players. They can respond dynamically to player inputs, demonstrate unique personalities, and adapt to gameplay changes.

4.2. AI-driven NPCs: An Insight into Their Creation

The design of nuanced, AI-driven NPCs involves a few essential steps: concept creation, design of visual elements, programming of behaviors, and ongoing refinement based on player interactions.

Firstly, developers conceptualize the roles and personalities of NPCs, drawing up profiles that detail their appearance, background, behavior, and role in the game's storyline. Next is the rendering stage where artists design and visualize NPCs. Following this is the most critical stage—programming NPC behaviors using AI.

This AI programming stage involves defining an "action-decision logic." This logic determines how NPCs react to various stimuli or shifts in the game environment. If traditionally this has been hard-coded, with actions following a decision tree model, AI enables a more dynamic and scalable approach.

AI algorithms, particularly machine learning and deep learning, allow NPCs to 'learn' from their environment and 'adapt' to situations. As such, behavior patterns emerge organically instead of being pre-scripted, fostering spontaneity and novelty in the gameplay.

4.3. NPC Personalities: Beyond Generic AI Behavior

AI permits NPC design to veer away from generic, robotic behavior towards distinct personalities. By leveraging Natural Language Processing (NLP), an AI subset, developers can create realistic dialogue for NPCs, which react differently depending on the player's communication style and decisions. This makes interactions more interesting, as each NPC conversation feels unique and meaningful.

NPCs with strong emotional depth can also be realized using AI. Emotional AI or 'Affective Computing' can be incorporated into the design, enabling NPCs to express and respond to emotions. The disposition of a character, whether being friendly, neutral, or hostile, can sway based on the player's actions. These emotion-driven NPCs are not just game progress devices anymore; they become characters with whom players can form virtual relationships.

4.4. Machine Learning and Deep Learning for NPCs

Advanced AI methodologies like reinforcement learning, a form of machine learning, have become instrumental in shaping NPC behavior. NPCs can learn from their actions and modify their behavior to achieve specific tasks, leading to unpredictable and dynamic gameplay.

Deep learning, another AI subset, is used to design NPCs capable of learning complex behaviors from data alone. Techniques like neural networks aid in understanding players' tendencies and evolving NPC behaviors accordingly. The higher the data volume absorbed by these layers, the better the NPC can interpret and react to player behavior.

4.5. AI-driven NPCs and Player Experience

The influence of AI-driven NPCs extends beyond gameplay and significantly impacts the player's experience. With their life-like personalities, NPCs can form more profound bonds with players. Players may even feel empathy for these characters, adding an immersive layer to the gaming experience.

AI-driven NPCs also spike the game's replayability quotient. As characters evolve and learn dynamically, playing against or with the same NPC can result in different outcomes. This unpredictability keeps gameplay fresh, entices players to return and discover new gameplay facets, enhancing overall game longevity.

Captivatingly designed AI-driven NPCs also contribute to strengthening the narrative depth, providing meaning, mood, and engagement. Their behavior can often create side-stories that diverge from the main plot, providing richer, more layered narratives that captivate the player.

4.6. In Conclusion

There is a powerful symbiosis between AI and the design of non-player characters in gaming. It fuels ever-evolving game design landscapes, allowing developers to push the boundaries of NPC design and interactivity.

AI has steered game design into a new era—an era where NPCs possess life-like qualities, react dynamically to player input, and learn from their actions. The application of AI in NPCs' creation has reinvented conventional philosophies of game design, modifying game narrative, complexity, and the overall player experience.

As AI continues to mature, the NPCs of tomorrow will be built with even more sophistication, emotional depth, and dynamism. The journey towards creating such responsive and intelligent NPCs chronicles an essential chapter in gaming history—reflecting a shift from strict pre-programmed lines to a fluid, AI-based narrative. This is not just creating more immersive gameplay; it's redefining the ethos of interactive entertainment.

Chapter 5. GameLand: How AI is Transforming Environment Design

The creation of a video game involves designing complex environments that immerse players into non-existent virtual worlds. Traditionally, designing these landscapes was a labor-intensive process, requiring a sizable team of designers and developers. However, the advent of AI is transforming environment design, introducing cost-effective and efficient mechanisms.

5.1. The Era of Procedural Generation

AI-sponsored procedural generation is an approach responsible for creating game content automatically. This method relies on highly sophisticated algorithms that generate large, diverse, and complex environments with minimal input from human designers.

For instance, games like 'Minecraft' and 'No Man's Sky' leverage procedural generation to create vast, engaging landscapes. This not only saves time and resources but also provides players with near-infinite, expansive environments to explore, a feat that would be virtually impossible for human designers.

However, procedural generation is not without its challenges. Although it can create endless landscapes, the algorithmically created environments sometimes lack originality and feel monotonously algorithmic. This is where AI steps in to augment procedural generation, infusing it with creativity and personalization.

5.2. The AI Perspective on Environment Design

By intertwining AI with procedural generation, expert systems can understand and emulate the creative process of human designers. They can create environments that are not just random but feel alive, brimming with creativity, and have a sense of purpose that seamlessly aligns with the game's narrative.

A crucial aspect of this AI-powered environment design is the use of machine learning. Deep Learning algorithms can study and learn the intricacies of good design principles by analyzing thousands of successful game maps and levels. They can identify patterns, understand how different elements interrelate, and create comprehensive rules that define efficient environment designs.

After acquiring this knowledge, the AI can generate new, intricate level designs that rival human-created environments in creativity and complexity. The generated designs can also be tailored to individual player preferences, thus providing a personalized gaming experience.

5.3. Customizing Environments: The Role of Player Behavior

AI serves as a powerful tool in customizing gaming experiences. It can understand and learn from player behavior within the game. Data from players' actions, strategies, and movements are analyzed to understand their preferences, skills, and gaming style.

Based on this analysis, AI can alter game environment elements in real-time to suit player's styles and intensify immersion. Elements such as terrain, atmospherics, and difficulty levels can be adjusted to ensure an engaging experience for individual players. For instance, if a player frequently uses stealth strategies, the AI might modify the light and shadow conditions to support more stealth-based gameplay.

5.4. Creating Adaptive and Dynamic Environment Designs

AI-driven environment design can also be adaptive and dynamic. Rather than remaining static, these settings respond to in-game events, enhancing realism. For instance, if a war zone environment is exposed to continuous artillery fire, AI algorithms can dynamically simulate the destruction, creating rubble, trenches, and craters over time.

This dynamism extends to the portrayal of natural processes. AI can recreate the changing seasons, day and night cycles, weather conditions, and growth, decay, or movement of flora and fauna. The effect is a world that feels alive, responsive, and encourages deeper player engagement.

5.5. The Power and Limitations of AI in Environment Design

Despite the immense potential AI holds for game environment design, it's important to take note of significant limitations and ethical considerations. While AI can generate detailed, expansive, and dynamic environments, there are concerns about originality and homogeneity. These systems learn from existing patterns, and thus, there might be a risk of designs becoming too similar or lack distinction that comes naturally with human creativity. There's also a risk of AI "creative decisions" diverging from a pre-planned narrative or game aesthetics.

AI surpasses human designers with its efficiency, cost-effectiveness, and ability to generate substantial, intricate environments. However, the human touch in designing game environments is irreplaceable as it adds soul and substance to the game world. Therefore, the future of game environment design is likely to be more about AI-human collaboration rather than complete AI domination.

To conclude, the interplay of AI in game environment design is an exciting development in the gaming industry. AI techniques not only ease the burden of manually designing environments but also bring a new level of personalization and immersion to gameplay. By understanding and embracing AI, we can create gaming experiences that are more immersive, exhilarating, and engaging than ever before. However, as we move forward in this journey, striking a balance between AI capabilities and human creativity will be the key to creating game environments that are just as irresistibly diverse and unpredictably imaginative as our real world.

Chapter 6. Teaching Machines to Play: Machine Learning and Gaming

Understanding the symbiotic relationship between machine learning (ML) and gaming provides insight into what makes games today increasingly compelling and interactive. AI algorithms, particularly machine learning, are at the heart of this transformation. Machine learning - a subset of AI - allows a system to learn patterns from data and make decisions with minimal human intervention. In the context of gaming, AI learns to respond to player actions or autonomously navigate an in-game environment.

6.1. The Inception of Machine Learning in Gaming

Machine learning in gaming isn't a new concept. It dates back to the era of classic games such as the 1951 Nimrod Computer that could play Nim, or IBM's chess-playing Deep Blue. In these early cases, the computer learned specific patterns and strategies essential to winning. The tradition of using ML in games has been evolving ever since, and the current era of gaming is witnessing a mind-boggling integration of advanced algorithms.

The 2013 machine learning breakthrough brought on by DeepMind with the Atari 2600 games kick-started a flood of research into the use of ML in video games. DeepMind's AI learned to play 49 Atari games just by "looking" at the screen and following the rules. This was a pivotal development that opened up limitless potentials for incorporating machine learning within video games.

6.2. The Significance of Machine Learning within Gaming

Enhancing Non-Player Character (NPC) behavior is one of the key areas ML has revolutionized. Older video game NPC's often had predictable behavior, and although some games had impressive AI, variability was limited. However, with the infusion of ML, NPCs have become more unpredictable; they can react dynamically to players and the environment, creating a more engaging experience. AI opponents can learn from each encounter with a player, adapting their strategies in real time, making games increasingly challenging.

Another crucial application domain for machine learning is game testing. Testing thousands of unprecedented permutations of a game is time-consuming and practically impossible for humans. Machine learning algorithms are ideally suited for this. They can tirelessly play infinite rounds of a game, in different ways, offering an excellent tool for locating bugs, balancing issues, or detecting exploitable game mechanics, therefore, ensuring a smoother user experience.

Additionally, ML empowers procedural content generation (PCG). Often, the dynamic elements of a game world, such as plants, animals, or weather, are procedurally generated to make the world feel larger and more realistic. ML algorithms can use PCG techniques to study player behavior, generate new content matching player preferences, and thereby, create more immersive game worlds.

6.3. The Use of Reinforcement Learning in Gaming

Reinforcement learning, a subset of machine learning, has shown considerable promise in the field of gaming as well. Reinforcement learning algorithms learn how to perform actions based on rewards and punishments, not unlike how humans and animals learn.

Using reinforcement learning, Google's DeepMind developed an AI known as AlphaStar that mastered the complex and highly popular game StarCraft II. The AI played and learned from a few supervised human games. Thereafter, the AI played against itself, gradually learning strategies that would provide it an edge over its competitors.

Such developments are exciting not just because they challenge the realms of what AI can achieve, but because it assists game developers in creating richer, more engaging gaming experiences for users at all skill levels.

6.4. Machine Learning Challenges and the Future

Despite all the excitement around machine learning in gaming, challenges exist. For instance, the training time for machine learning algorithms is often long and requires immense computational resources. Also, it can be hard to define objectives and rewards, especially in games with complex mechanics or open-world environments.

Moreover, creating truly versatile AI agents is a tall task. Often, AIs trained in one environment perform poorly when moved to another. However, research into transfer learning, where an AI uses knowledge gained in one setting to navigate another, is an exciting development that shows promise in overcoming this limitation.

As machine learning becomes more integral to the gaming experience, the future of gaming will undoubtedly be deeply entwined with the development of AI. This fusion of machine learning and gaming holds tremendous promise for the creation of unimaginably immersive, complex, and personalized gaming experiences. The journey is just beginning, but the progress thus far hints at the endless possibilities for the interplay of AI and games, and the consequent revolution that awaits the future of gaming.

Chapter 7. A New Reality: Emergence of VR and its Interplay with AI

The journey to a new reality started with the birth of video games, which for decades, operated as two-dimensional or three-dimensional on-screen experiences. Immersion was limited to what could be represented on a flat screen. However, the emergence of Virtual Reality (VR) has completely redefined the concepts of immersion and gameplay in the world of video games.

VR provides the ultimate experience of "being in the game," transforming players from spectators to active participants. To ensure that the promise of this technology is fully exploited, AI has emerged as an essential ally. The combination of VR and AI is creating an incredibly rich and immersive gaming experience beyond anything previously imagined.

7.1. The Birth of Virtual Reality Gaming

Virtual Reality began its journey in the gaming world in the early '90s with pioneering systems like the Virtuality Group arcade machines and the Nintendo Virtual Boy. Despite offering a novel experience, these early efforts were held back by the technology of the time. Clunky equipment, simplistic graphics, and a lack of engaging content meant that VR was not yet ready for mass adoption.

Fast forward to the present, and VR has witnessed remarkable advancements in both hardware and software. Devices like the Oculus Rift, HTC Vive, and PlayStation VR have brought VR gaming to households worldwide, allowing players to immerse themselves entirely into new, breathtaking realities.

The immersion these devices offer goes far beyond what standard flat screen games can provide. You're not just playing a game, you're transported into the world of the game. Whether you're exploring fantastic realms, solving puzzles or engaging in combat, the game world envelops your senses, and your actions directly affect that world.

7.2. AI and VR: A Symbiotic Relationship

AI's role in video games has historically been to control non-player characters, deciding their actions based on pre-programmed scripts or certain triggers during gameplay. However, the advent of VR has given AI a new purpose—to make these virtual worlds more believable, more interactive, and above all, more immersive.

The AI algorithms used in VR environments help create a seamless interactive experience. By analyzing vast amounts of data about player behavior, AI can manipulate the virtual environment and adjust the game's dynamic elements to adapt to the user's actions, creating personalized experiences unique to each player.

Simulation games using VR and AI lead to higher levels of immersion. For example, games that simulate flight, racing, or space exploration engage the player more deeply by leveraging AI to respond appropriately to the player's actions. This combination of technologies can also be used to train individuals in a variety of practical applications beyond gaming, such as pilot training or medical surgery simulation.

7.3. Rise of AI-Enhanced NPCs in VR

Creating lifelike NPCs poses a substantial challenge for VR developers. Virtual humans must not only look real, but they also need to behave and react realistically for players to accept them as believable components of the virtual environment.

AI is being used to create intelligent NPCs that can interact meaningfully with players. The NPCs are designed to perceive the player's actions, understand them, and react accordingly in real time. Machine learning algorithms help these NPCs adapt and learn from every interaction, allowing for more complex and dynamic interactions as the game progresses.

Proximity-based interactions are another area where AI is making significant impact in VR gaming. NPCs can now respond to a player's movements or the distance between them. For example, getting too close to an NPC might make it step back, enhancing the realism of the game world.

7.4. VR and AI: Revolutionizing Game Design

Just as AI and VR are changing gameplay, they're also revolutionizing game design. With VR, game designers have a whole new level of freedom and creativity. They're no longer bound by the 2D plane of a screen; instead, they can create fully interactive 3D worlds. With AI, they can make these worlds dynamic, reactive, and personalized.

AI is also helping to automate the game design process. Procedural generation techniques are being used to create vast and varied virtual landscapes, while machine learning algorithms are aiding in the design of complex gameplay mechanics.

This new reality of game design that combines groundbreaking hardware and intelligent software challenges the traditional norms of video games, and promises incredible possibilities for the future.

7.5. Conclusion: The Future Reality

The combination of VR and AI gives us a glimpse into the future of video gaming. While we are only at the start of this exciting journey, the prospects are limitless. We can expect more lifelike, immersive experiences, with dynamic game worlds that adapt to our actions, creating a unique, personal journey for every player.

As VR and AI technologies continue to advance, we will see the lines blur between the physical and virtual worlds. In a not-so-distant future, we might arrive at a reality where the gaming experience is so immersive and interactive that we can't tell where the real world ends, and the game world begins.

The marriage of AI and VR is more than just an infusion of two separate technologies - it's a symbiosis that is redefining the boundaries of gaming, creating a new world of virtual realities where we're no longer just players, but active and integral parts of the gaming universe.

Chapter 8. The Mechanisms Behind AI-Driven Game Development

AI has revolutionized the gaming industry by serving as the backbone for a variety of dynamic experiences. It helps in creating complex game scenarios, enhancing the player experience, and providing a platform for designers to achieve their creative visions. This section will delve into the mechanisms behind AI-driven game development, exploring techniques, applications, and implications of AI in the industry.

8.1. AI Techniques in Game Development

Game development relies heavily on AI, which is achieved through different techniques:

Machine Learning (ML): ML, a subset of AI, enables computers to learn from data without being explicitly programmed. In gaming, ML techniques such as reinforcement learning have been used in games like Dota 2 and StarCraft II, allowing the AI to devise strategies by playing millions of matches.

Neural Networks: Neural networks are models inspired by the human brain. They can adapt and learn over time, providing an excellent mechanism for creating intelligent NPCs (Non-Player Characters). By using neural networks, developers can create NPCs that can adapt to player's actions, making the gameplay more engaging.

Genetic Algorithms: These algorithms imitate natural evolution. In gaming, they are used to create dynamic and adaptive environments based on player input.

Natural Language Processing (NLP): NLP allows games to understand, analyze, and generate human languages. It's essential for interactive games featuring dialogue and decision-making, like narrative-driven RPGs.

8.2. Applications of AI in Game Development

Non-Player Characters (NPCs): AI drives the behavior of NPCs. Traditional techniques involve decision trees, state machines, or rule-based systems. However, AI advancements have allowed for complex behavior modeling, making NPCs that respond intelligently to the game environment and player's actions.

Procedural Generation: This refers to creating game content algorithmically, enabling unlimited and dynamic game worlds. AI can adapt these worlds based on player behavior, facilitating a unique gaming experience every time.

Game Testing: Testing is crucial for game development. AI enables automated, exhaustive testing by simulating players and rapidly discovering potential issues.

Personalized Gaming Experiences: AI can track player's in-game behavior, adjusting difficulty, storytelling, and game mechanics in real time to cater to individual playstyles.

8.3. Implications of AI in Game Development

AI has several implications within the gaming industry:

Cost and Time Efficiency: AI reduces the effort and time required to generate content. Using AI reduces development costs and enables faster release cycles.

Improved Graphics: AI assists in generating high-quality game graphics, making for more immersive experiences. NVIDIA's DLSS (Deep Learning Super Sampling) uses AI to upscale lower-resolution images in real time, providing higher-quality visuals with less performance impact.

Realism: Artificial intelligence allows developing lifelike NPCs, enhancing realism and immersion. NPCs can learn from interactions, making their behavior more unpredictable, engaging, and human-like.

Constant Evolution: AI-driven games can evolve over time, adapting to trends, and player feedback, maintaining player engagement.

8.4. Challenges in AI-Driven Game Development

Despite its potential, AI-driven game development has challenges:

Complexity: AI models used in games can be complex and computationally heavy, requiring significant resources to implement.

Unpredictability: While AI can enhance gameplay by adding unpredictability, it can also lead to unforeseen and potentially undesirable outcomes.

Balance: Striking a balance between too much and too little AI is tricky. While abundant AI can mean a more immersive experience, it might also risk overwhelming the player.

The implications and applications of AI in game development are vast and continually expanding. And while there are challenges involved, dedicated research and innovation promise a future wherein AI could be the most influential mechanism driving game development. AI continues to breach the boundaries of what is thought possible in games, marking the dawn of a new era in the gaming industry.

Chapter 9. The AI Influence: Understanding User Experience in Gaming

While user experience in gaming has historically been a demanding domain, often relying on intensive manual design and high-concept artistry, the advent of artificial intelligence has ushered unprecedented transformations. AI technologies are reshaping the way we approach user experience, employing sophisticated algorithms, machine learning and automation to turn even the most complex experiences into digitally rendered, playable realities.

9.1. How AI Powers Immersion in User Experience

Immersion—the feeling of being completely involved or engrossed—is a critical aspect of user experience in gaming. By offering gamers a plausible, compelling world to explore, games command attention and stimulate emotional investment. The key to fostering this level of immersion relies heavily on artificial intelligence technologies.

Creating a believable world isn't just about stunning graphics and intricate gameplay mechanics—it entails the creation of a dynamic, self-evolving system. Game developers employ AI to generate realistic Non-Player Characters (NPCs) which react authentically to player actions, and to the events of the game world. These NPCs are embedded with natural-language understanding and can generate humanlike responses, enabling deeper player engagement.

Moreover, AI algorithms allow for the design of adaptive game universes that react to player choices. These procedural generation techniques enhance world-building and narrative progression, making the gameplay experience unique and unpredictable. As a result, every player is immersed in a personalized adventure that feels distinct and immersive.

9.2. The Role of AI in Individualizing Gameplay

One of the most exciting capacities of AI in gaming revolves around personalization. AI technologies can learn from player behavior—gleaning information about preferences, play style, skill level, and even emotional response to various game elements.

Through machine learning, developers can create games that adapt to the player. These game algorithms modify challenge levels, manipulate enemy behavior, tweak puzzle difficulty, and orchestrate narrative arcs to align with the individual player's gaming approach. By catering the gaming experience to the user, AI-induced personalization enables more engaging and enjoyable gameplay.

For instance, a novice player may encounter fewer, less challenging enemies initially, allowing them to acclimatize to the game's mechanics before the difficulty ramps. Simultaneously, experienced players can be engaged right at the onset with more challenging obstacles, ensuring they do not lose interest due to lack of difficulty.

9.3. AI-Enabled Emotional Engagement

But AI's influence on user experience isn't merely restricted to immersion and individualization. Perhaps the most crucial yet imperceptible role AI plays is in manipulating the emotional engagement of players.

Behavioral tracking and sentiment analysis allow AI to intuitively read and respond to player emotions. By analyzing tells such as pacing, reaction times, facial cues (where available), and patterns of movement, an AI system can craft emotional beats in the game to create a dynamic rhythm of tension and relief. This can amplify the thrill, suspense, and sense of achievement, contributing to a more memorable game experience overall.

9.4. AI's Pivotal Role in Reducing Routine and Manual Tasks

AI also contributes significantly to enhancing the user experience by tackling routine tasks effectively. Pathfinding AI, for instance, can guide players in expansive game environments, enhancing navigation and reducing the potential for frustration. Intelligent bots also take over repetitive tasks, providing players with more time to enjoy the more engaging aspects of the game.

9.5. Fair Play and Enhancing Spectator Experience with AI

In multiplayer settings, AI plays an instrumental role in ensuring fair play by monitoring gameplay for signs of cheating or inappropriate behavior. With machine learning, AI systems become progressively better at spotting anomalies and rule-breaking actions. This not only improves the overall player experience but also makes the game a safer and more inclusive space.

Additionally, AI impacts the experience of those who observe games rather than play them. Esports, for example, benefits from AI-enabled features such as automatic highlight generation, real-time strategy prediction, and analysis that enriches the spectator experience, making it more engaging and interactive.

By enhancing immersion, personalizing gameplay, enabling emotional engagement, reducing mundane tasks, and ensuring fair play, AI is distinguishing itself as a game-changer in the gaming industry. As AI technologies continue to evolve and mature, we can expect even deeper and more meaningful transformations in the user experience of gaming, offering us a glimpse into an exciting future of interactive entertainment.

Chapter 10. Ethics in AI Gaming: Balancing Innovation and Fair Play

Human exceptionalism, the belief that we are different and superior to all other animals, has a profound impact on our decisions and interactions. Now, as AI continues to weave its way into our day-to-day lives, posing new ethical dilemmas, we're forced to reevaluate this belief. It's no different in the sphere of video games, where NPCs powered by AI have become exponentially more intelligent, providing nearly human-like interactions. This dramatic progression prompts further discussion and scrutiny about the boundaries of AI in games.

10.1. The Moral Status of AI in Games

It's hard to assign moral status to video game characters. They don't feel pain, they don't have thoughts or emotions, and they certainly don't have rights. Or do they? With the advent of AI and increasingly realistic NPCs, it's a question that warrants contemplation.

Consider a story-based game in which an NPC is subjected to violence. The character reacts with realistic fear and distress. Knowing the interaction is with an AI, does that absolve us of any moral responsibility? Would it change your actions if a character you'd been interacting with for a game's entirety suddenly pleads for mercy in a concretely human way? Is it immoral to cause distress, even if the recipient of that distress is an AI? This is a highly contentious issue with valid points on both sides. Some argue that NPCs lack consciousness so our interactions lack ethical dimensions. Others posit that even simulated suffering should be avoided, empathizing with the artificial pain the AI experiences.

Developers also play a key part in this moral constellation. Their responsibility doesn't end once a game is sold; they have a continuing duty to ensure that their AI does not facilitate harmful experiences or behaviours.

10.2. Balancing Competition and AI

AI also presents ethical challenges in competitive multiplayer video games. Should AI be allowed to compete with humans? How do we maintain a sense of fair play when AI has the potential to be far more competent, fast, and precise than any human could be?

This applies to the use of AI bots, which have been known to skew competition in online multiplayer games. Developers need to ensure balance; they must make the game enjoyable and challenging for both human and AI players. If the AI becomes too strong, gamers will likely lose interest due to the perceived lack of fairness.

Moreover, accessibility should be maintained throughout the game. Innovative AI shouldn't lead to an unnecessarily complex gaming environment that only a few can navigate effectively.

10.3. AI and Data Privacy in Games

In AI-driven gaming, data is a double-edged sword. On one hand, data gathered about players help create personalized experiences that cater to individual preferences, behaviors, and even emotional responses. On the other hand, this level of data collection presents serious privacy concerns that developers must responsibly manage.

While implementing machine learning algorithms, it's crucial to anonymize data to protect players' identities. Developers must be forthcoming about their data collection and usage, to maintain trust with their users. Legal regulations such as General Data Protection Regulation (GDPR) are in place to protect users, but these require careful consideration and vigilant enforcement.

10.4. Exploring Bias in AI

AI within games is created by humans. This means it is susceptible to bias, raising concerns about perpetuating stereotypes and discrimination, however unwittingly. From the design of characters to narrative decisions, developers need to ensure that AI isn't building unfair or biased virtual worlds.

For instance, if an AI is coded to learn from players, it quite possibly could absorb and implement biased behaviours based on the actions it observes. This could inadvertently result in the reinforcement of harmful stereotypes or actions. Developers have a responsibility to guard against such occurrences, both in the initial stages of AI design and in ongoing monitoring and adjustment.

Understanding the complexities surrounding ethics in AI gaming is no small feat. It's a nuanced issue that demands conscientious consideration and continuous examination. As advancements continue to impel the boundaries of gaming, developers must shoulder the responsibility of ensuring they are making ethically sound decisions, achieving a balance between innovation and fair play. The integrity and future of the gaming industry depend on it.

Chapter 11. The Future Landscape: Prospects and Challenges in AI-Driven Gaming

Modern gaming is virtually unrecognizable from its early forms—what began as two square paddles and a dot in the game Pong, has evolved into incredibly detailed virtual universes where players can live out numerous thrilling adventures. At the forefront of these innovations in artificial intelligence. Whether employed subtly or overtly, AI has persistently been pushing the boundaries of what's possible in the gaming arena.

11.1. The Evolution of AI in Gaming

In the early days, the AI in gaming was a collection of simple rulesets programmed to react to player input in specific ways. The aliens in Space Invaders would drop faster the more you destroyed, the ghosts in Pac-Man had determined paths, and the enemies in Mario games had straightforward action-response scripts.

However, as technology advanced, game developers began leveraging it to create more immersive experiences. The late '90s and early 2000s saw the rise of games where non-player characters (NPCs) showcased behaviors governed by ingenious AI systems. The NPCs in the popular JRPG series, "Final Fantasy," would conduct themselves based on a gamut of parameters, and the marines in "Halo" would react to player tactics dynamically.

Later, with the advent of machine learning algorithms and neural networks, games became even more sophisticated. NPCs started learning from player behavior, tracking commonly used strategies, and reacting to them accordingly. Procedural content generation began to be used, leveraging AI to produce unique game scenarios for every playthrough.

11.2. The AI Revolution in Game Design

One area where AI has exerted a strong influence is game design. Traditionally, game experiences were explicitly designed by human developers; every aspect, from the environment to character behavior, was painstakingly handcrafted. This method, although effective, was often time-consuming, resource-intensive, and couldn't guarantee a unique experience for different players.

This is where AI stepped in. Advances in computing power and machine learning algorithms have fostered a new era of dynamic and personalized game design. Game developers now harness AI to generate content procedurally, including environments, storylines, and character behaviors. This has given birth to games like "No Man's Sky," where an entire universe, teeming with unique planets and species, is generated procedurally.

AI is also redefining the concept of immersive story-telling in games. It's now possible for games to tailor their narrative based on the decisions and actions of the player. The game world evolves with the player, creating a dynamic, compelling experience.

11.3. Improving Player Experiences with AI

Beyond game design, AI is also enhancing player experiences in numerous ways. Machine learning algorithms employed in matchmaking systems create balanced and fair player versus player environments by predicting player skill levels and matching them accordingly.

AI has also made strides in curbing toxic behavior in online gaming platforms. Games now incorporate systems that can analyze player chat and actions, flagging and sanctioning toxic behavior. This has made environments safer and more enjoyable for players.

AI is even making games more accessible. Whether it's text-to-speech technology helping visually impaired players enjoy games or systems that adjust game difficulty based on player proficiency, AI is reducing barriers to gaming.

11.4. Future Perspectives: Promising Developments

Looking ahead, AI-driven gaming has even more to offer. The rise of advanced machine learning techniques, such as deep learning, promises to catapult gaming to new lofty heights. Deep learning can be leveraged to engineer more complex, fluid NPC behaviors and create exceedingly vast, lifelike virtual environments.

One of the exciting developments on the horizon is the use of AI to enable enhanced player-NPC interactions. Future games may feature full conversations with NPCs, with the NPCs having their distinct personalities and knowledge base.

There's also a potential for an explosion of AI in the realm of virtual and augmented reality gaming. Using AI, developers could create realistic, interactive environments and responsive characters, providing an immersion level like never before.

11.5. Challenges on the Horizon

However, the future of AI-driven gaming isn't without obstacles. One prominent challenge is the so-called "AI effect." With any incremental advance in AI, what was once considered AI soon becomes seen as merely a part of the software's programming, leading to diminishing recognition of AI's role in driving innovation.

Another challenge is the balance between AI-driven dynamic game environments and explicitly crafted human-led experiences. Striking the right balance between the two is vital to ensuring the continued evolution of engaging video games.

Issues related to privacy and security, particularly in online gaming environments, are other potential stumbling blocks. With AI systems collecting and analyzing vast amounts of player data, safeguarding that data is a paramount concern.

11.6. Looking Towards the Future

The convergence of AI and gaming has delivered some of the most enthralling experiences in contemporary entertainment. As the technology continues to evolve, games promise to become more immersive, characters more engaging, and stories more absorbing, than ever before. Equipped with unprecedented tools and possibilities, developers are plunging into an era of unparalleled creativity and invention, and at the heart of it all, stands artificial intelligence. Despite the challenges lying ahead, cybernetic frontiers in gaming look more exciting than ever. Gaming isn't just about play anymore - it's about creating, learning, experiencing, and growing in a virtually boundless world conjured through artificial intelligence.

9 798856 365800